FAMILY

⟫⟫⟫ TIME ⟪⟪⟪

Andrew Brannigan

CONTENTS

HOW TO USE THE BOOK

Nothing just happens. The experiences we want our children to have, the values and beliefs we want them to hold and the relationships we want them to cherish come about when we are purposeful and deliberate. When we teach beliefs and build relationships with children. If we don't do it, it won't just happen. For God's command is to:

"Love the LORD your God with all your heart and with all your soul and with all your strength. These commandments that I give you today are to be on your hearts. Impress them on your children. Talk about them when you sit at home and when you walk along the road, when you lie down and when you get up." **Deuteronomy 6:5-7**

So this book is a starting point! It contains suggestions for praying with children and devotion outlines. These look at significant occasions, moral and life lessons and some of the basics of Christian faith. The intention is that parents, grandparents and other family members will use it with all children–but it may fit best with five to ten year olds.

Please note that the devotions can be dipped in and out of (you don't have to do them all!) and suggestions on how to use them will be on the following pages.

Some things to think about to help you get the most out of these prayers and devotions.

You don't have to be an expert. These are basic prayers and devotions making simple points for children about life and faith. You do not need to have a strong faith or Biblical knowledge to lead them.

The material is adaptable. Outlines are simple with enough information for each devotion so feel free to add and take away as you deliver it. For instance the 'Talk' part does not have to be just read out word for word.

Finding the right time and place. The prayers can be used on a daily basis or every few days while the devotions will probably work best on a weekly or fortnightly basis. For devotions, sitting round a table works well for some families.

Preparation. Most activities only need a few minutes thought but you will need to read over the devotions in particular before you do them (some activities will need practiced!).

Improvising. The activities, discussion, talks and so on will all need to be improvised from time to time to suit your circumstances so don't be afraid to do this.

Regularity. As much as possible try and do them at the same time and place to help build up a routine. Find a good routine that will not be easily broken.

Get a Bible. It is possible to do the devotions without a Bible as the key verses are printed but to get the best use out of it you will need a Bible. This is especially useful if the children are old enough to read the verses for themselves. Also it is worth buying a child or family friendly Bible (not Bible stories). The NRSV version of the Bible is used for memory verses here but you should buy one that best suits you.

Have fun! Use the activities especially to have some fun, give out some treats and so on. There is a serious side to this learning but the children should also enjoy it.

THE SABBATH

For many families the role that a Sunday Sabbath plays is key to their devotional time. We are commanded to treat the Sabbath specially and here are some suggestions for doing this:

Make it the best day of the week:

Eat the best food (Sunday is traditionally a feast day), save up treats for Sunday, go out together, stay in together, play games together and just sit around–together!

Rest:

Work harder on a Saturday to rest on a Sunday. No housework, homework, shopping and odd jobs. Do as little as possible and don't feel guilty. Rest, its Monday tomorrow.

Adapt your Sabbath:

Some families might want to reflect a sundown to sundown approach–taking the Sabbath from Saturday evening to Sunday evening to allow for work on Sunday night in preparation for Monday.

Enlist help:

The whole family should help as they can to make the Sabbath special. Such as helping with Sunday dinner and various other tasks that may fall to just one person!

Every time you see this symbol, there is a verse or statement that can be memorised.

MEMORISING BIBLE VERSES

Why? The Bible is full of commands from God for us to study and follow His Word. In an age where we can look up the Bible on our phones it can seem unnecessary for anyone to memorise verses. However it is just as important as it ever was. Verses that are memorised will guide a person, protect them from harm, prompt them to do good and remind them to pray. As a child grows up these verses can often come into their minds just when they need something to refer to–including times when their parents are not there to advise them.

These devotions and prayers can be done without any element of memorising and they will still be useful. However, they are a great opportunity for children to learn things that they may remember for the rest of their lives. It is a lot easier for children to memorise than you might think and even something as long as the Ten Commandments can be memorised by children as young as six years. A good age to begin memorising is around five to six years.

HELPFUL TIPS FOR MEMORISING

1. Small steps:

The most basic way to learn verses is to take small steps by breaking up one line or verse (up to around twenty words) into two or three sections. For instance by breaking up the following verse in to three sections:

'Accept one another, then, | just as Christ accepted you, | in order to bring praise to God.

Say the first part and get the children to repeat it until they know it. Then do this for the second part. Combine parts one and two together until learnt. Then learn part three before combining all three parts of the verses together.

2. Repeating:

Over the next week or two try and ask for the verse every day at a regular time (such as dinner or bedtime) and have the verse handy to you so that you can prompt them.

3. Recapping:

As you use the devotions try and recap on verses previously learnt by saying the first few words. You might be surprised by how well they do.

4. Learning Passages:

For longer ones such as the Lord's Prayer it may take months to learn but the process is similar. Learn one line, repeat it over the next week or two, learn the second line and repeat lines one and two together over the next week or so. Then do this for the third line and so on.

5. Don't do too much:

Try not to overload the children and yourself! If it is proving too hard to learn the verses it may be that the children are too young or that you are doing too much. You don't have to learn a verse each week even if you are doing the devotions each week. For instance you could learn one verse over three weeks of devotions and simply not memorise the other two verses.

6. Other ways to memorise:

Display it: You could have the verse written or printed out for the children to read. It could be decorated with pictures/drawings related to its theme and displayed on a fridge/cupboard as a reminder.

Act it: Many verses can have simple actions put to each part in order to prompt children in remembering it.

Sing it! If your child struggles to memorise or is younger then it may help to put a verse to an easy tune such as a nursery rhyme or kids' song. This isn't as hard as it sounds!

Finally, Children can often memorise well but not actually understand the verse that well. This is fine. The verse will be in their memory for a day in the future when they will understand it better.

PRAYING WITH CHILDREN

We know that teaching prayer is essential for passing on faith to children but this means modelling what prayer is too. Church prayers and Sunday school are a great help but children will have a different understanding of the importance of prayer when their family prays. They will realise over time that if their family is not praying then faith is not taken seriously. And if they do not grow up with prayer they will eventually question why they should do it for themselves.

Some thoughts on praying with Children:

Children see the world in simpler ways than adults. Their prayers will often be simple and short.

Children have less experience than adults. We should not expect them to pray and relate much beyond ideas about family and school life. Over time encourage their thinking and praying beyond this–such as praying for people in other countries.

Children love to talk and ask questions! The importance of this time together is also about the talk before and after the actual prayer. So discussion on how the day was and topics for prayer is good–as well as listening to stories from their day and questions that they may have.

Children need routine. It would be great if your prayer time becomes a habit that both you and the children are used to doing every day (or most days) or it can easily be forgotten. And like all good habits, if you stop for a while, don't let that put you off starting again.

WHEN AND WHERE TO PRAY:
Find some set times and places that are part of your daily life. Mornings are a possibility but tend to be a rush for many families. Dinnertime is also an option if you don't have people going out afterwards. Bedtime is a third option and one that tends to suit most families as there may already be a routine for bedtime in place and prayer is a simple addition to this. Where to pray should be part of a routine were you have your prayer time in the same place as much as possible. Suggestions include round a table, in a spare room or living room or on a bed. You don't need a routine to pray–it just helps.

A SAMPLE PRAYER TIME:

SETTLING IN: Help children to calm down and settle for prayer by gathering them in an attentive position (where it is not easy to run around) and perhaps reading a story. It should also be clear that, as this is prayer time with God, good behaviour is expected.

TALKING: About what was good and bad about the day, hearing their stories and then applying this to the prayers. For example the 'teaspoon' (tsp) prayer:
Thank you: What could they thank God for?
Sorry: What do they need to say sorry for?
Please: What could they ask God for?

PRAYING: They could close their eyes and put their hands together for prayer (it helps them not to be distracted) and could pray either sitting, lying down or kneeling. As a suggestion each person could begin their prayer with 'Dear God', 'Heavenly Father' or 'Dear Lord' and finish with 'Amen'. The prayer could include a 'thank you', 'sorry' and 'please' as a sample structure. You could also encourage them to ask for prayer requests for you to pray and also offer prayer requests that they could pray for you.

APPEARANCE

1 SAMUEL 16:7

 Play a 'what's changed' game. Get some hats, gloves, scarves, sunglasses etc and get the children to close their eyes while you see what you can do to change your appearance. You could add a hat, change your hair, change how your shirt is buttoned and so on. Then, to finish, change nothing at all about your appearance and when they guess that nothing has changed say that you 'changed your mind' about something.

 What is easiest to notice, things that we change in our heads or changing how we look? Why do you think people try to look and dress well (to be liked, to impress, to be respectful)? Sometimes people can concentrate too much on the outside and then forget what is on the inside–our good thoughts and good deeds and the love we have for others. Always remember that God is most interested by what goes on in the inside–not how we look.

"People look at the outward appearance, but the LORD looks at the heart." **1 Sam 16:7**

Father God, thank you for loving everybody no matter how they look and for seeing beautiful things about everyone. Help us to be good people on the inside, so that we can become more like your Son Jesus every day. Amen.

BEING WORRIED

PHILIPPIANS 4:6-7

Send the children for a quick walk upstairs or to the furthest part of the house. Then put on them a lot of heavy clothes–jackets, over-trousers, boots and adult coats– until they are really weighed down! Then go with them to repeat the journey they just made. Keep the clothes on while you do the talk.

 Which was the easiest of the two walks and why? Which of the clothes was heaviest? Now what do you think a worry is? A worry is when you keep thinking about something that could go wrong–like when you could be told off or getting lost or not having friends. Being worried is like walking with all those heavy clothes on as it makes you tired and weighs you down. The important thing with worry is that you tell someone about it and tell God about it. This helps to take the worries off you (take off their heavy clothes) so that you feel better.

"Do not worry about anything, but in everything… let your requests be made known to God" **Philippians 4:6**

Dear God, sometimes it's hard not to worry. Help us to talk to you when things are good and when things are bad. Amen.

OBEDIENCE

EPHESIANS 6:1-3

 'Opposites' game. The children have to do the opposite of what you ask. For example if you say 'sit down' they must stand up. Other examples could be to: 'Open your eyes, whisper hello, stand still, keep your tongue in, hold out your right hand, cross your arms etc'.

SAY Sometimes children do the opposite of what their mum and dad ask don't they? They might be asked to be quiet and what happens? Or to go to sleep and they stay awake. What other things do children do that is the opposite of what they are asked? God says that children should obey their parents because it pleases him. Do you know why? Because he has given you to your mum and dad as a gift for them to take care of and to teach. So for parents to do this well they need you to try and be obedient and do what is asked–even when sometimes you don't want to.

 *"Children, obey your parents in the Lord, for this is right".* **Ephesians 6:1**

PRAY Father in heaven, thank you for everybody who cares for us. Help us to listen to them and love them, in the way that you want us to. Amen.

BEING THANKFUL

1 THESSALONIANS 5:16-18

 Ask if they can think of ten things to be thankful for today and allow around sixty seconds thinking before asking each person to try and name them. Make the point that this can be hard to do. Then tell a story of a child in a poor country, perhaps having the same sort of day. They might have no comfortable bed, no electricity, breakfast, no sink or inside toilet, TV, toys, shower.

SAY How would you feel if we did not have some of those things that we use every day? What would you miss the most? We are very fortunate to have them aren't we? This is why it is important not just to say 'thank you' every time we are given something (like a present or sweets) but to be thankful for all the things that God has already blessed us with.

 *"Rejoice always, pray without ceasing, give thanks in all circumstances."* **1 Thessalonians 5:16**

PRAY Thank you, God, for everything you give us. We're sorry we sometimes forget to say thank you. Amen.

DOING YOUR BEST

HEBREWS 12:1-3

 Place a prize for a child somewhere in the room that they can get to. Then have a competition for each child separately to try and get the prize–but that they have to get past you. Gently prevent them from doing this but just before they start to get frustrated pretend to be distracted so that they can get it. Congratulate them and repeat this appropriately for other children.

 You did very well because even though you could not get the prize at the start you did not give up and did get it in the end. Did you feel like giving up? God says in the Bible that the most important races are not the quickest ones but the longest ones–where you have to keep going even when you feel like giving up. Some things need us to keep on going and doing our best–like learning in school and at home, looking after others and following God. God says that if we run the race to do these things then we will win a great prize.

"...and let us run with perseverance the race that is set before us, looking to Jesus, the pioneer and perfecter of our faith"
Heb 12:1-2

Thank you God for the prize you promise us. Be with us as we run your race, trying every step to come closer to you. Amen.

BEING TRUSTWORTHY

LUKE 16: 9-11

 'Faith falls'. Ask the child to cross their arms, keep their legs straight and slowly fall back into your arms. Start with very small falls by catching them just as they overbalance and perhaps build up to something more exciting by falling back off a chair–be reassuring and safe!

Was it hard to do this? Why or why not? Would you like anyone to catch you? Why or why not? To let someone catch you they have to be trustworthy. Trust is doing what you say you will do and not cheating or lying. People that can be trusted are very good people and God says that if you can be trusted with small things to do then he will give you much better things to do.

"Whoever is faithful in a very little is faithful also in much; and whoever is dishonest in a very little is dishonest also in much"
Luke 16:10

Dear God, we can trust you for everything we need. Make us more like you, so that others will know they can trust us. Amen.

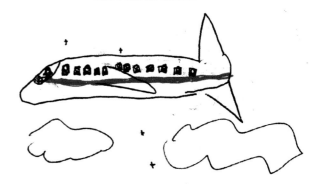

BEING SCARED

WHAT is FORGIVENESS?

JOSHUA 1:9

PLAY!
Blindfold each child and ask them to make their way from one part of the house to the other–one at a time. Be with them to help keep them safe but help them as little as possible–they need to feel that they are on their own. Once they are done or have given up try it again but this time walk beside them and give them instructions.

SAY
What was the easiest way to get there and why? Was it a little bit scarier by yourself? What are some of the things that we are scared of (the dark, spiders, large dogs, etc)? It is OK to be scared of things–especially if they are dangerous. And the best thing to do when you are scared is to get someone to be beside you (like the second walk) but also to ask God to be beside you because he will never leave us.

"Be strong and courageous; do not be frightened or dismayed, for the Lord your God is with you wherever you go." **Joshua 1:9**

PRAY
Loving God, thank you that you are with us wherever we go. Remind us of this, especially when we feel like we are lost and don't know where to go. Amen.

PSALM 103: 8-12

PLAY!
Get a couple of blank pages and draw a rough picture of something people do that is wrong (a fight, angry face, dropping litter, making a mess etc). Get a child to get rid of the wrong by scribbling it out. Give them around 10-15 seconds to do this.

SAY
Does scribbling out the wrong make it look better? Is the wrong picture still underneath? It hasn't gone away has it? When we do something wrong it doesn't go away either and can't be covered by other things. The only way to get rid of our wrongs is to say sorry and ask to be forgiven. When we do this God takes the wrong things (hold up scribbled picture) and throws it away (put it in the bin) and lets us start again. This means we are like a brand new page again to start anew (give out clean blank page).

"as far as the east is from the west, so far he removes our transgressions (sins) from us." **Psalm 103:12**

PRAY
Brilliant God, no matter how many bad things we do we know you will forgive us. Help us to change, so that we live our lives the way you want– so that everyone will know you have forgiven us. Amen.

FEELING UNSETTLED

WHY WE ARE SPECIAL

JOHN 14:27

 Do a 'run-around' game throughout the house. Each child should be given a series of tasks to do, one after the other, to get them busy and tired out. If there is more than one child get them to do different tasks at the same time. Examples could include: switch on/off the TV, flush the toilet, bring a cushion/pillow, ring the door bell, get a spoon, count the stairs, get a toothbrush and so on. Do this until they are out of breath. Then sit them down and do a series of deep breaths to get them settled again.

 Did that feel very busy and tiring? What was the hardest task? What did we do then to settle ourselves to feel better? When do you feel the most busy (in the mornings, school, homework etc)? Sometimes when we are busy it is important to get some peace and settle ourselves down by stopping for a few moments. Getting some peace is a good thing. God can give us peace too—but his peace is with us all of the time, even when we are really busy.

"Peace I leave with you; my peace I give to you... Do not let your hearts be troubled and do not let them be afraid." **John 14:27**

 Thank you, God, for hearing us even when we aren't speaking. Amen.

PSALM 139:13-14

 Get something about the size of an apple and tell them that this was their size just as their fingerprints were being finished in their mother's tummy. Then look at each person's fingerprints and see if they are the same. You could do this by making an impression of fingerprints on some blu-tac or by breathing on a window and pressing on the condensation.

 Every single fingerprint is different. So even though we can look similar to the people around us there is no one else in the world just like you. You were created by God as special—but not only that, he created you to do special things—like being able to help and love your family, friends and others in ways that no-one else can. You are special because you were created special and because there are special things for you to do.

"For it was you who formed my inward parts; you knit me together in my mother's womb" **Psalm 139:13**

Dear God, you know us better than anyone. Thank you that you know everything about us and love us. Help us to love other people the way you love us. Amen.

TALKING + LISTENING

PROVERBS 12:15

PLAY! Communication games. Make up a few sentences and whisper them at a distance to see if they can be heard. Read out the opening verses with the radio or music playing loudly to see if it can be heard. Then get everyone there (including yourself) to say what they have done today–all speaking at the same time. Or ask a child some questions but each time interrupt their answers!

SAY How hard was it to hear what was being said each time? Why was it hard? Sometimes we need to think to be able to listen well or else we don't hear it or forget what was being said (and then perhaps don't do what we were asked to do). It is important that when someone talks to you that you try and listen but it is also important for them to listen to you–and this is especially important for families. God always listens to us, no matter what we say, but we should remember to talk to him.

 "Fools think their own way is right, but the wise listen to advice" **Proverbs 12:15**

 PRAY Dear God, thank you that you always listen to us, no matter what we say. Help us to listen to other people better. Amen

WHEN WE SAY WRONG THINGS

EPHESIANS 4:29-32

PLAY! Get the children to try and repeat the following tongue twisters as quickly as possible: "She sells seashells on the seashore", "Peter Piper picked a peck of pickled peppers, where's the peck of pickled peppers Peter Piper picked?"

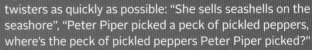

SAY It is very easy to not say things the way we want to isn't it? We often say the wrong thing or speak without thinking and hurt someone's feelings. What are some examples (an insult, complaint, gossip, laughing at someone, saying someone is bad at something or you are better, bad words and so on)? The Bible says that even our little tongues can do a lot of harm to others and so to try and be very careful about what we say.

 "Let no evil talk come out of your mouths, but only what is useful for building up, as there is need" **Ephesians 4:29**

 PRAY Dear God, you are good in every way. Help us to want good things for others, and help us to find kind things to say to people. Amen.

WHAT IS LOVE?

1 CORINTHIANS 13: 4-7 & 13

 PLAY! What are the different ways in which we can show someone that we love them? That you have perhaps seen in family life, on TV and so on? (A hug, kiss, helping someone up, comforting someone, a loving look, saying 'I love you', doing something for another and so on). If possible try and act some of them out!

SAY Love is a lot more than saying 'I love you' isn't it? It is also a lot more than a kiss or a hug. Love is about helping others, being patient, sharing things, taking care of someone and making them feel better. Love is especially important in families but it is something that we should try and show to others as well. The Bible shows us just how much God loves us (so much so that God's son, Jesus, died for us). The Bible also reminds us that we should love God back and love other people.

"And now faith, hope, and love abide, these three; and the greatest of these is love." **1 Corinthians 13:13**

 PRAY Loving God, thank you for the people who love us and that you love us more than anything. Help us to love you and show love to others. Amen.

BEING HAPPY

JOHN 10:7-11

PLAY! Put a small empty glass on a plate and place beside it a bowl of water, jug of water and dessert spoons. Place them all on a towel. What makes you happy (treats, trips, being with others, doing good, etc)? For every happy thing that is described take a spoonful of water and pour it into the glass. Do this for several answers but don't fill the glass to the top.

 SAY The glass is like our lives, and each time something happens to make us happy it starts to fill up our lives. But every time a sad thing happens (like an argument, hurt, etc) it can take some water out (do this by taking a few spoonfuls out). God has promised that he can fill us up with so much that our lives overflow with good things (use the jug as 'God' to overflow the glass)–and all this happiness overflowing can be given to others.

"The thief comes only to steal and kill and destroy; I have come that they may have life, and have it abundantly." **John 10:10**

 PRAY God, nothing can make us happier than knowing you. Help us to know you more every day, so we can become happier in every way. Amen.

FORGIVING OTHERS

EPHESIANS 4:29-32

 PLAY! Place a small glass in a basin or large bowl and place a jug of water beside the basin. Get a bit of dirt from outside and place it in the glass. Ask how we might get rid of the dirt without touching it or the glass. Then pour the water in from a height and it should wash out the dirt.

SAY Whenever someone does something wrong it is like adding a little bit of dirt into their life. And this dirt is not something that we can get rid of by ourselves. To do this it is important for us to ask for forgiveness from a person when we do something wrong to them. This is why it is important to say sorry to people and for them to be able to say 'that's OK' or 'I forgive you'. But for all things that we do wrong it is important to say sorry to God–and when he forgives us he washes the wrong things right out of our lives.

"be kind to one another, tender-hearted, forgiving one another, as God in Christ has forgiven you." **Ephesians 4:32**

 PRAY Dear God, thank you that you wash the wrong things out of our lives. Lead us to be kind and loving to others, and to forgive them. Amen.

BEING A FRIEND

ROMANS 15:7-8

PLAY! Go through the different ways to say 'hello' in the languages below. Get the children to try and say them and then to guess what countries might use these ways to say hello.

Bonjour	France
Guten Tag	Germany
Kon-nichiwa	Japan
Shalom	Hebrew/Israel
Hola	Spain

SAY Every part of the world and each type of person has ways to say 'hello' and to be friendly. But what else do you need to do to be a friend (ask names, be nice, smile, be truthful, play together etc)? Sometimes it can be that no-one plays with us or we don't seem to have friends but if we are a good friend to others then we will eventually get friends–and don't forget that God, even though we can't see him beside us, is always there as our friend.

"Welcome one another, therefore, just as Christ has welcomed you, for the glory of God." **Romans 15:7**

 **PRAY** Dear God, you see every person as the same. May we be accepting to others, so they can see your love. Amen.

HELPING OTHERS

MATTHEW 25: 37-40

 PLAY! Do a short quiz to ask what sort of people are helped by various professions. For instance a firemen would help someone in a fire or accident. You could include a fireman, nurse, policeman, mechanic, coastguard, minister, home help etc. Ask what they might like to be when they grow up.

SAY Some people have jobs where they are supposed to help other people who are in trouble or are sick but all of us are supposed to help out other people when we can. How might we help out other people in our family or in school? Also, don't forget that there are times when we might need help ourselves and it wouldn't be nice if no-one helped us would it? This is why God says it is important to help others.

"Truly I tell you, just as you did it to one of the least of these who are members of my family, you did it to me." **Matthew 25:40**

 PRAY Loving God, thank you for people in our lives who help us. Help us to be kind to our families and friends. Amen.

LIVING + CREED

2 CORINTHIANS 9:6-8

PLAY! Gather together as many denominations of money that you can find from small coins through to banknotes. Ask which one has the most value. Then put the money into various combinations in 2 or 3 piles and ask again which one is worth the most. Then ask a few questions about how much money might be needed to buy some everyday things like a bar of chocolate or a meal for the family.

 SAY How much do you think it might be to buy another person–perhaps to buy a mum or dad? Do you think you can? You can't buy people because they are more important than money. However, you can buy things that can be given to people. What can we buy that could help or bless others (presents, holidays, trips, food, clothes etc)? The Bible says that because we have been given good things we should give to others that are in need and not try and keep everything for ourselves or get more for ourselves as this is being greedy.

"the one who sows sparingly will also reap sparingly, and the one who sows bountifully will also reap bountifully." **2 Cor 9:6**

 **PRAY** Lord God, you have blessed us with lots of good things. We want to bless others by sharing the things you have given us. Help us to do this. Amen.

FAIRNESS

DEALING WITH PROBLEMS + SADNESS

MICAH 6:8

PLAY! Gather around ten small 'treats' such as sweets, biscuits etc and place them on a table. Then ask if you should share them out. When you do make sure that they are counted into uneven amounts for each person (you could include yourself) depending on the amount of people. Ask the person with the most if they are happy with their amount and ask the same of the person(s) with the least. Then take the treats back and say you will give them out again at the end (evenly!).

SAY It is often not fair to give out more to some than others isn't it? What would be a fair way of giving out the treats? With lots of things that happen to us it often does not seem fair—perhaps someone gets something better than you, or gets more than you. Sometimes there is just nothing that we can do about unfair things that happen—but we can do something about how we treat others and God asks that we try and be fair to others.

 "and what does the Lord require of you but to do justice, and to love kindness, and to walk humbly with your God" **Micah 6:8**

PRAY Dear God, Help us to be happy as we try to be fair with others. Amen.

PSALM 55:22

PLAY! Get a bucket and lots of heavy objects such as stones, tools etc. Ask the children to lift the empty bucket. Then explain that each time we have a big problem or are very sad it can add a big heavy weight into our lives. Mention times when we are lonely, in trouble, scared, worried, and so on and add a weight for each one. Then see how hard it is to lift the bucket.

SAY Everyone has times when they have problems and are sad. When we don't get help with problems and sadness it can make our lives harder—the way that the bucket got heavier. But when we share these problems with God and with our family then they can help remove some of them (remove some weights) so that we can be lightened again. This is why God always says to give our problems to him.

 "Cast your burden on the Lord, and he will sustain you" **Psalm 55:22**

PRAY Lord God, it is amazing that when we are sad and when things are going badly, you are with us. May we remember to always bring our problems to you. Amen.

WHAT WE CAN BECOME

PSALM 139:13-16

 **PLAY!** Get a photo of each child as a baby and ask what things they can do now that they couldn't do then (walk, talk, dress themselves etc). Then show a photo of yourself as a child (preferably around their age) and list some of the things that you couldn't do at their age (that perhaps they can!) but emphasise the things that you have learnt and done up to now. Talk about some of your milestones/achievements as a child, young person and adult.

 SAY There are many things that you have not learnt yet and that you cannot do. But as you grow up God has a plan for you to learn and do some exciting and important things—and no one knows yet what they are. If you keep learning and trying and ask for help from your parents, teachers and others, but especially from God, then you will become a person that can do very important things.

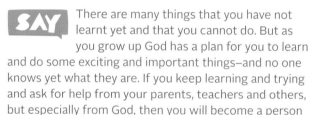 *"In your book were written all the days that were formed for me, when none of them as yet existed."* **Psalm 139:16**

 PRAY Father God, you see not just who we are but who we will be. Help us to keep learning from others, and from you, so we will grow up to be the best people we can. Amen.

ARGUING

2 TIMOTHY 2:23-25

 PLAY! Play a yes/no game. Ask the children lots of quick fire questions about their day, favourite things, TV, games, school etc and throw in lots of questions that are usually answered yes/no. The aim is for them not to say 'yes' or 'no' or to hesitate too long.

 SAY We often get into arguments when someone says 'yes it is' or 'no it isn't' don't we? What are some other reasons for arguing (blaming someone, thinking they are wrong, tiredness)? Even grown-ups argue! The Bible says to not argue over silly things, because you can fall out easily, and to remember to say sorry when you do. If we don't say sorry after arguments then we can lose friends and upset our family.

 *"Have nothing to do with stupid and senseless controversies; you know that they breed quarrels."* **2 Timothy 2:23**

 **PRAY** Lord God, we don't want to argue and fight over silly things. If we do say or do things we shouldn't, help us to say sorry. Amen.

WHAT TO DO WHEN WE ARE ANGRY

WHEN WE DONT THINK WE CAN DO MUCH

JAMES 1:19-20

PLAY! Go for a walk around the house but include 'pretend' traffic lights. As they walk, if you shout 'Red' they have to immediately stop. On 'Amber' they have to get ready to start and on 'Go' start walking again.

SAY What gets us angry (examples from your life as well—not being listened to, an accident, people shouting etc)? What are some of the things that can happen when we are angry (lose temper, get upset, hit someone, say the wrong things, cry etc)? Do we feel good when we are angry? How do we feel? God asks us to try hard to get rid of anger and a good way to do this is to use the traffic lights. As soon as we are feeling angry to stop (red), think about something else for a minute (amber) and then start again (green) and this should help us to feel less angry.

 "let everyone be quick to listen, slow to speak, slow to anger" **James 1:19b**

PRAY Dear God, when we are angry and want to say bad things, help us to take time to pause and think; take our anger away in those moments, so that we don't say or do the wrong thing. Amen.

1 PETER 4:8-11

PLAY! Get a pencil and paper and draw an outline of a hand for each person present (including yourself). Make the point that each hand is different. Now have a quick discussion on agreeing five encouraging things to describe each person there and as you do write one inside a finger on each outline. (e.g. helpful, funny, smiley, obedient, comforts, artistic, school work, takes care of sibling, music, sports, tests, friendly, cares for others etc).

SAY God made every person and even little babies with gifts that they can give to others. Not like giving presents at Christmas but things that we can do every day to help others and make them feel good. You have lots of things that you can do well—like being kind, saying nice things to others and obeying your parents. And these things are all needed by your family, friends and teachers to help them.

 "...serve one another with whatever gift each of you has received." **1 Peter 4:10a**

 Dear Father God, thank you that there are things we are good at. Help us to use the gifts you give us to help and care for others. Amen.

DOING OUR SCHOOL WORK

COMFORTING OTHERS

GALATIANS 6:9-10

PLAY! What are the hardest and easiest things that we do in school? What are the most enjoyable (Maths, English, spellings, tables, science, art, computers, games, sport etc)? Share with them the things that you liked most and least from your school days at their age.

SAY Some things in school are much harder to learn than others (share an example of what you found difficult). But you can still do well with the hard parts of school if we keep trying and ask the teacher to help us. You should also ask your parents for help. God can help us too–not to give us the answers for homework, but to help us try our best–and that is all that we need to do.

"So let us not grow weary in doing what is right, for we will reap at harvest time, if we do not give up." **Gal 6:9**

PRAY Lord God, we want to try our best in everything we do. When this seems too hard, help us to keep putting in effort in all our life, especially at school. Amen.

2 CORINTHIANS 1:3-4

PLAY! Imagine that a sibling/cousin/ friend was in the house with us today and that they were very sad and were crying. What would you do to comfort them (hug them, get someone to help, give them a hanky, cup of tea, give a present, ask what is wrong and so on)? What do you think might happen if you were to leave them alone and not comfort them?

SAY It doesn't feel nice when we are sad and upset and it is always good to have someone try and help us. God says that this is what we must do with others, even when they sometimes say 'go away'. It is important because comforting others is another way of showing that we love and care for people.

".. so that we may be able to console those who are in any affliction." **2 Cor 1:4b**

PRAY Thank you, God, for people who help us to feel better when we are sad. Help us to be caring and loving with people we know, especially when they are sad, so that we might be able to help them feel better. Amen.

FINDING IT HARD TO DO THE RIGHT THING

CARING FOR THE WORLD AROUND US

EPHESIANS 2:8-10

PLAY! Hold your arms out straight in front of you with the palms of your hands facing each other. Raise one arm and lower the other. Tell the children that they have to clap as soon as your two arms cross past each other. Do this a few times and then try it by stopping your arms from crossing at the last moment. The children will probably miss this and still clap.

SAY Sometimes it can be easy to do the things we don't want to do (the hand clap game) and hard to do the simple things we want to. What are some of the good or right things that we find hard to do (tidying up, school work, going to bed, sharing, praying)? God knows that we find it hard to do these things but he tells us not to give up. He promises us a reward if we keep trying to do what is right.

 "For we are what he has made us, created in Christ Jesus for good works, which God prepared beforehand to be our way of life." **Ephesians 2:10**

 Dear God, help us to do the things that are really important, and to never give up– especially because we know you will help us. Amen.

COLOSSIANS 1:15-17

PLAY! Prepare a rubbish bag that you should put some 'clean' rubbish into like plastic, card and so on. Before you start reading the verse say that you forgot to sort out the rubbish and then make a big play of throwing the rubbish all over the garden (or kitchen floor). Ask them if they think this is what we should do with the rubbish. Then ask where it should really go and then go and put it there.

SAY Why shouldn't we throw rubbish anywhere? What if it was only small sweet wrappers? How do you think we should take care of the nature around us such as plants, rivers and animals (less rubbish, being tidy, planting trees, feeding birds and so on)? The Bible says that God made everything in the world, including us, and that he said that it was good. It is therefore important for us to try and take care of Gods creation.

 "for in him all things in heaven and on earth were created," **Colossians 1:16a**

 Dear God, thank you for the wonderful world we live in. Please remind us in our lives to look after the great things you have created. Amen.

BEING LONELY

DEUTERONOMY 31:6

PLAY! Play a camera phone toy hunt. You'll need to spend a few minutes hiding some toys around the house and then taking a photo (making it as hard as you like) of each hiding place on a camera phone. Then explain to the children that the toys are lonely and that they will need to use the photos on the phone to find them,

SAY Why would the toys have been lonely? What stopped them being lonely? When do you think people get lonely (no friends, new to something, friends not able to play with them etc)? God has given us family and friends and we are very blessed, but people can have times when they are just by themselves and feel lonely. These are occasions when we should ask if someone needs a friend because some day we might need a friend too.

 "Be strong and bold.. because it is the Lord your God who goes with you; he will not fail you or forsake you..." **Deut 31:6b**

PRAY Father God, it is so good that no matter where we are or what we do we are never alone because you are with us. When we see people who are lonely, help us to be brave enough to talk to them and be their friends, because you are always our friend. Amen.

MONEY

2 CORINTHIANS 9:6-7

PLAY! Put a banknote in front of everyone and ask them what they think it might buy. Give some answers from your own experience. Then ask what they think it might buy in a poor country such as in Africa. As an example, in Central Africa most households bring in less than $10 per day to get by. Then ask the children what they think are some of the things that money can't buy (families, love, friends, laughter etc).

SAY Money is important because it buys food to eat, clothes to wear and a house to live in. But that also means that it can buy good things for other people too. God says that it is important to give to others as well as looking after ourselves because they are God's children as well.

 "for God loves a cheerful giver." **2 Cor 9:7**

PRAY Dear Lord God, no matter how much or how little we have, help us to be generous to other people, because you made us all and love us all. Amen.

HOW TO THINK GOOD THOUGHTS

NOTICING DIFFERENT PEOPLE

PHILIPPIANS 4:8-9

 **PLAY!** Get two clear plastic bags and then prepare two piles of items to place on the table. One pile should consist of rubbish and the other of valuable or useful things such as a favourite toy, pen, phone, food etc. Explain that every time we do a good deed or even read about or watch good things then it is like filling our minds up with something good that can be used again (fill a bag with the useful things). However, if we watch and read a lot of bad or stupid things (especially on TV) it can fill our minds with rubbish (fill the other bag with the rubbish). What bag would you rather be like?

Often the things we watch on TV or read about are not **SAY** very nice–it could be fighting, people being bad to each other or scary things. If we watch these things too much then they fill our heads up with rubbish and are not good for us. This is why God tells us to be very careful about what we let into our lives and minds and why parents do not let children watch certain programmes on TV.

"..if there is any excellence and if there is anything worthy of praise, think about these things." **Philippians 4:8b**

 PRAY Dear Lord God, you made a world full of good things for us to fill our minds with. Help us to be strong and look for only good things to enjoy. Amen.

GALATIANS 3:26-28

PLAY! Ask them to think of all the children in their class at school and to list some of the things that they have in common (uniform, shared liking for toys, programmes, movies, sports, music etc). Then ask them to think of some of the differences that there are between everyone in their class (height, size, colour, eyes, voice, hair, personality traits, abilities etc). What are some of the other differences that people have (different ages, languages, colours, backgrounds, disabilities and so on)?

SAY God makes us very alike but also very different. He doesn't want everyone to look and sound the same and do the same thing. God wants us to be different from each other so that we can remember that he created us special. That is why we have different eyes, hair, faces, height, colour, voices and abilities. And God loves them all. And he asks us to love them all too.

"for in Christ Jesus you are all children of God through faith." **Galatians 3:26**

 PRAY Loving God, thank you that everyone in the world is different– it would be so boring if we were all the same!! Just as you love everyone, no matter what they look like, help us to love everyone in our lives just like you love us. Amen.

WHEN WE GET INTO TROUBLE

1 JOHN 1:8-9

 PLAY! Explain that you are going to be their 'controller'. Stand behind them and walk them about, then use their arms to make a mess or to gently 'hit' someone. Do things to generally get them into trouble! Do this for each child.

SAY How do we often get into trouble? (fighting, not doing as we are told, breaking things etc) How do other children we know get into trouble? Have you ever wanted to blame someone else for something you have done? Has anyone ever made you do something wrong? When we do wrong it is important to realise when it is our fault and not to blame someone else. The best thing to do when we get into trouble is not to hide it but to own up to it and say that we are sorry.

"If we confess our sins, he who is faithful and just will forgive us our sins..." **1John 1:9a**

PRAY Lord, when we get things wrong or do bad things, help us to be good and brave and own up and say sorry. We know there is nothing you will not forgive – but we want to be more and more good as we live our lives. Help us not to do bad things, so that we don't have to apologise too often! Amen.

DEALING WITH PEOPLE THAT ARE BAD TO US

MATTHEW 5:43-45

PLAY! Act out some different ways in which people can be bad to us. It could be the things we say ('I hate you!'), things we do (not letting someone be involved) or the looks that we give to others (try lots of 'mean looks'). Which ones would make you feel the worst?

SAY People can do bad things to each other. What are some examples (hurting, stealing, making them cry, not being a friend)? Sometimes they will be very bad to us and it is very important to get help from a parent or teacher when this happens. However God still loves people, even when they are bad, and we should remember to pray for them, forgive them and try to be good to them –and this might help them to stop being bad.

"But I tell you, love your enemies and pray for those who persecute you" **Matthew 5:44**

PRAY Loving God, sometimes it is hard to like and care for people who aren't very nice to us. We know you want us to love these people too. Help us not to return their bad behaviour with badness of our own; instead, give us enough love to pray for them. Amen.

CREATION

ALL HAVE SINNED

GENESIS 1:1-5

PLAY! Try and find a map of the world or a globe and put it in front of everyone (this could still be done without a map). Ask about people they know who have travelled to different countries, find them on the map and talk about how far away these places are, what they are like, how they might have travelled and so on. Then talk with them about their favourite places more locally. Why do they like these places?.

SAY In the beginning God created the whole earth—mountains, seas, deserts, icecaps, fields and everything. He made places that are far away and he made where we live. God also made the plants and animals, fish, insects and people. God was very pleased with the people he created. Do you know who the first two people were (Adam and Eve)? God also created you and me and he people everywhere. There is nowhere in the world we can go to where he will not be. God will always be with us.

 "In the beginning God created the heavens and the earth." **Genesis 1:1**

PRAY Lord God, everything good in the world came from you. You made the world, and you made us with real love and care. Thank you for your world; thank you that you are still in the world and with us in everything we

do. Amen.
ROMANS 3:23

PLAY! Place a glass of water on the table and ask one person to taste it and see if it is pure (drinkable). Explain that the first people were created pure but then sin (disobeying God, doing, saying and thinking wrong) came into the world. Sin spoils our lives like dirt spoils water. Ask for some examples of sin and each time you get one add a drop of soy sauce or similar to the water. After several examples the sauce will have discoloured the water. Ask if anyone wants to taste it now.

SAY God created the world, and the first people, perfect. There was nothing wrong with it. But Adam and Eve disobeyed God by eating from a tree in the Garden of Eden that they were told not to. This was the first wrong thing (sin) and it meant that all people were separated from God and couldn't be with him because he has no sin. Every person now has sinned and is like the water that has gone brown and we can't mix it with God, who is like pure water. But God had plans to make us pure again (next devotion).

"Since, all have sinned and fall short of the glory of God" **Romans 3:23**

PRAY Father God, we know that sometimes we fall short of the standard you set for us. We thank you that, despite this, you will have a plan to make us pure again. Help us to remember this as we live our lives. Amen.

JESUS CHRIST

JOHN 14:6

 PLAY! Camera phone treasure hunt. Hide a prize in a part of the house/garden and take a picture of the location on a camera phone. Then put a pass code on the phone and write the code on a piece of paper that has 'Jesus' written on the other side. Place the paper somewhere obvious. Explain that there is a treasure hidden somewhere for them but that the clue to where is on a picture in the phone. Give them the phone to unlock and once unsuccessful ask them who the verse says is the 'key' to being with God in heaven. Encourage them to find the paper with 'Jesus' on it and from that find the treasure.

SAY We are separated from God in heaven because of our sin so God's plan was to send his son, Jesus, who was without sin, to live with us. When Jesus died he was able to defeat sin and death and everything that is bad. This means that Jesus is the only way for us to get to be with God again, and to have a place in heaven.

"I am the way and the truth and the life. No one comes to the Father except through me."
John 14:6

 **PRAY** Dear Jesus, it is brilliant that you have given us a way to God. Because you gave your life for us, we can have a relationship with God. Amen.

REPENTANCE

LUKE 15:8-10

 PLAY! Hide several coins (real or chocolate!) around the room(s) and spend a few minutes letting the children search for them. You can give clues by saying 'warmer' or 'colder' to help the search go quicker!

SAY Have you ever lost something that you really liked? Did you go and look for it? How did you feel when you found it? How do you think you would feel if you were lost yourself? Would you want to be able to see your mum or dad? We are sinners. This means we are lost. Whenever we don't do what God wants and do wrong things it is like being lost and not being able to see God. (When we do this we are called 'sinners'). But God comes and finds us just like the woman did with the coins. When God finds us, if we say sorry for the wrong things we do (repent) and try to do good things, then he is really happy (rejoices). In fact, not just God, but the angels in heaven are happy and glad when we do good.

"..there will be more joy in heaven over one sinner who repents than over ninety-nine righteous people who need no repentance."
Luke 15:7

 **PRAY** Dear God, we're sorry when we are disobedient and do the wrong things. Thank you that you love us and forgive us. Please help us to do the right things. Amen

25

FORGIVENESS

1 JOHN 1:8-10

PLAY! Before you begin the reading go and get your hands really dirty. Then do the reading (with your hands hidden if possible) and ask the children if they will hold hands with you for prayer. If they see your hands and are reluctant ask them why (perhaps they don't want to get dirty too). Also ask if you should prepare food, clean or help with homework with hands like this. What should we do with them? Then clean your hands.

SAY Whenever we sin it is like a little bit of dirt getting attached to us and it also means that we cannot be beside God as he cannot have sin in his presence–a bit like you not wanting to hold my hand because it was dirty. However, if we say sorry and turn away from our sin to God God forgives all our sins, now and in the future, and makes us clean again. This means that we will get to be with God in Heaven, no matter what happens we will always be with God. This is forgiveness.

 "If we confess our sins, he who is faithful and just will forgive us our sins and cleanse us from all unrighteousness." **1 John 1:9**

 Thank you, God, for forgiving me and being with us always. Amen.

FOLLOWING JESUS

MATTHEW 4:18-20

PLAY! Get a map of the country and point out where you live in it. Ask if they can remember where their friends and relatives live and see if you can find these places on the map. Also try and find places that you have visited, favourite places and places that you might like to go to. You could also point out rivers, mountains and so on.

SAY When we become a Christian we are followers of Jesus. This means that we don't just follow where he might take us but that we try and follow or obey what he asks us to do. We try and be like him. It will mean, for instance, that we still go to school–but that we try and do what Jesus wants for us while we are there. What might that involve (being friendly, telling the truth, trying hard to learn, telling others about Jesus, helping etc)? This is what it means to follow Jesus, trying to do what he wants every day.

 "And he said to them, 'Follow me, and I will make you fish for people." **Matthew 4:19**

 Help us, Lord God, to follow you every day more and more, and as we follow you to learn more about doing the things you want every day. Amen.

HOLY SPIRIT

ACTS 1:8-9

PLAY! Find the lightest 1-ply tissues that you can and place one per person on the floor. Then ask how we might move the tissues across the floor without touching them with anything. Each person then races the tissues across the room by putting their face close to it and blowing. Make the point that even though we didn't touch the tissue, and we couldn't see how it moved, we know that our breath did it.

SAY Sometimes it is really hard to do the right thing–we try to be good but we sometimes end up not being good. Can you think of any times that this might happen (when tired, when you forget, when others are doing something they shouldn't)? God knows that we find it hard and so he sent his Holy Spirit to help us. The Holy Spirit is God's power on earth and he can help us to do the right things. Even though we can't see him or touch him he can still help us (just like how we moved the tissue).

 "But you will receive power when the Holy Spirit has come upon you; and you will be my witnesses.. to the ends of the earth."
Acts 1:8

PRAY Father, we can't see your Holy Spirit, but we know he is there because he hears us when we pray. Thank you that your Holy Spirit means you are always with us. Amen.

WHAT IS PRAYER?

1 THESSALONIANS 5:16-18

PLAY! Explain to the children that you are going to ask them if they would do some tasks for you–but only by using signs and actions. For instance to close/open a door, bring you a biscuit, bring a pillow, give you a drink of water etc. Do each task one at a time and help them if they aren't doing well.

SAY Prayer is about talking to God. It means we can tell him anything we want at any time in any place and all day long if we want. And the amazing thing is that God wants to hear us. Even if we don't know what to say to him, or how to say it, even if no one else understands us, God does understand us and how we feel. So it is very important to try and talk to God.

 "Rejoice always, pray without ceasing, give thanks in all circumstances;"
1 Thessalonians 5:16-18a

 Lord God, thank you for our friends that we enjoy talking to. Help us to remember that the most important person to talk to is you. Amen.

27

HOW TO PRAY

COLOSSIANS 4:2

 PLAY! Ask someone to say a short prayer or read out the verse above but each time they start find a way to interrupt them–scrape a chair back, cough, talk to someone and so on. Then ask one more time but before they start turn on a radio or some music. Ask how it feels to be interrupted. Then let them finish without interruptions.

 SAY It is important to pray but we need to remember that prayer is not just talking to any person-it is talking to God. So we need to try and concentrate and not interrupt other people when they are praying to God. A simple way to help us concentrate and teach us how to pray is to remember to say:

Thank you: For what God provides for you and good things that have happened today.
Sorry: For what you have done wrong.
Please: For the things that you want to ask God to do. *This can be easily remembered by the acronym t.s.p (teaspoon).*

 "Devote yourselves to prayer, keeping alert in it with thanksgiving." **Colossians 4:2**

PRAY *Ask the children to think of one thing to thank God for, one thing to say sorry for and one thing to ask him for. Fit them in to the simple prayer below.*

Dear God, thank you for....
We are sorry for/that/when...
We ask that...
In Jesus' name. Amen.

READING THE BIBLE

MATTHEW 4:1-4

 **PLAY!** Go and get some children's Bible story books and give them a bit of time to look through some and pick their favourite story and why. You should also share your favourite Bible story.

SAY The Bible is God's story to us. It tells us about how God made the world and everything in it, how he provided for people and why and how we should follow Jesus. It also tells us what God is like–what pleases him, what makes him cross and how much he loves us. So it is really important that we read the Bible to find out about God and how to be a Christian.

"One does not live by bread alone, but by every word that comes from the mouth of God." **Matthew 4:4**

PRAY Thank you, God, for all the fantastic stories we know. The story of your love is the most amazing. Help us to take time to read your word in the Bible so we can learn more about you. Amen.

WORSHIP

JOHN 4:23-26

PLAY! List as many different aspects of church life as you can and each time ask the children to do some actions to see if they think the aspect of worship life is UP towards God (Point your hands up), IN towards helping us (put your hands on your heart) or OUT to help others (arms out wide). If an aspect is two or all three of these things then use all the actions. For instance the singing may be mostly 'UP' but also 'IN', a fundraiser may be 'OUT'. Other aspects of church can be the welcome, prayers, announcements, sermon, reading, offering, creeds, children's talk, confession, communion and so on.

SAY Because God has created everything and is so good to us, it is important that we worship him. This means praising and thanking God—and just enjoying being in his company. There are lots of ways to worship God and in a church service it could be singing, praying, reading and so on but there are many ways to worship God outside of church too. For instance by learning about God (like this time together) and by following him we are worshiping too.

 "God is spirit, and those who worship him must worship in spirit and truth."
John 4:24

PRAY Heavenly Father, you are wonderful in every way. Help us to take time in Church, in school, with friends and on our own, to worship you by praying, by learning and by telling you how much we love you. Amen.

GUIDANCE

JEREMIAH 29:11-13

PLAY! If you were lost and didn't know how to get home what are some of the things that you might do to get guidance home (asking for directions, phone, use a map, sat-nav, road names, ask a bus driver etc)? Can you think of some of the things that people would have done a long time ago to help guide them (Sextant, compass, stars, nature and so on)?

SAY Guidance isn't just about finding a place—it is also about being guided to do the right things. It is very easy for us to do what we want to do and not follow God. And sometimes we want to follow God but don't know what we should do! Well God has wonderful plans for our lives and he wants to guide us. But Christians don't use a sat-nav or map for guidance—we pray, read the Bible and ask other Christians for their help in following God and doing the right things.

"I know the plans I have for you, says the Lord, plans for your welfare and not for harm, to give you a future with hope."
Jeremiah 29:11

PRAY Dear God, thank you that you have wonderful plans for all your children. Help us to know you better through praying and your Bible, so that we can find out all the good plans you have for us. Amen.

TAKING LITTLE STEPS

DOUBT

PSALM 119:101-105

 PLAY! Play 'rotten tomatoes'. Get lots of smallish soft toys or else lots of crumpled up newspaper. Explain that each toy/paper is a rotten tomato and that you are going to throw them at them. If a rotten tomato hits someone they will get into 'trouble' for having tomatoes on their clothes. The give them a five second start and get throwing!

SAY Sometimes it can be hard to avoid things that get us into trouble and sometimes we want to be good but end up being naughty. God knows this and he knows we will get into trouble. However, he is prepared to forgive us. Adults get it wrong all the time as well. So God wants us to try and take little steps–where we try to do little things every day to please him and others. What could some of these things be (smile, help someone, be a friend, do a job, say 'thank you')? The lamp in the verse gives light to people's feet–their next steps. God wants us to think about the next steps.

 "Your word is a lamp to my feet and a light on my path." Psalm 119:105

PRAY Dear God, we want to be able to take little steps to live better lives. Show us the way as we do this so that we don't get lost. Amen.

PROVERBS 3:5-8

 **PLAY!** Explain that you are going to blindfold someone and then ask them to sit down gently on a chair. Once they are blindfolded and ready to sit down make a big deal of promising that the chair will not be taken away (you could also promise this before the blindfold is on). Then move the chair a bit so that it sounds like it has been removed. Then see if they will sit down. Once finished ask if they doubted if it would be OK, even though you promised that it would be (and was).

SAY Even though God can do anything, and even though he loves us so much, we can still doubt if he is there and will take care of us. Why do you think this is (can't see him, can't hear him speak, a prayer not answered the way we want)? God knows that we sometimes find it hard to believe but he says to ask him for faith (which is believing even if we don't see) and he will give us faith.

 "Trust in the Lord with all your heart, and do not rely on your own insight." Proverbs 3:5

 **PRAY** Lord God, when we find it hard to remember that you love us so much and that you can do anything, give us more faith to trust in you with all our hearts. Amen.

BEING AN EXAMPLE

MATTHEW 5:14-16

 PLAY! Meet in a room that can be easily darkened by drawing curtains etc. Have a torch or phone with a light. Then ask how many potential sources of light there are in the room (such as the main lights, electrical appliances, toys etc). Then, with the main light on, switch on the torch/phone and ask how bright your light is. Do it again after darkening the room and ask if your light is brighter. It is the same light but why does it seem brighter?

SAY Jesus said that we are to be like light to the world around us—that our lives should be lights. Now sometimes it doesn't seem like we notice this light but other people will. And the darker, or more difficult, that things are for people the more our light can shine into their lives to help them. This light isn't like a torch but it is Jesus living in us and when people see Jesus in our lives it can bring light to their lives. How do you think we might be a light to others (by trying to follow Jesus)?

 "let your light shine before others, so that they may see your good works and give glory to your Father in heaven." **Matt 5:16**

PRAY Dear Lord, help us to live our lives in a way that shows other people how good you are. Amen.

FRUIT OF THE SPIRIT

GALATIANS 5:22-23

 **PLAY!** Play a quick-fire 'reveal quiz' with various fruits. Gather below the table and out of sight as many fruits or tins of fruit that you can find. Reveal them one at a time very quickly and see how long it takes to get the right answer. The quicker you are the more wrong answers you will get!

SAY Sometimes it doesn't seem like we are doing lots of good things but remember that God sent his Holy Spirit to help us. The Bible says that as we follow God and grow as Christians we will start to bear fruit—just like a fruit tree does, as it gets older. But the fruit that we will produce will be the good things that will help us and other people—like love, joy, peace and kindness.

 "the fruit of the Spirit is love, joy, peace, patience, kindness, generosity, faithfulness, gentleness, and self-control." **Gal 5:22-23a**

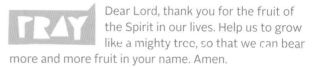 **PRAY** Dear Lord, thank you for the fruit of the Spirit in our lives. Help us to grow like a mighty tree, so that we can bear more and more fruit in your name. Amen.

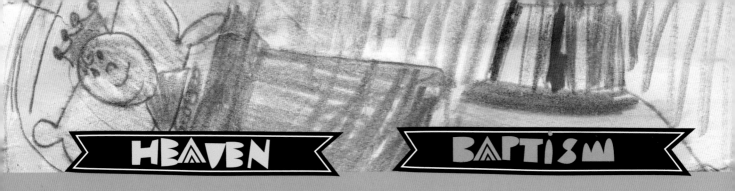

HEAVEN

BAPTISM

JOHN 14:1-6

PLAY! Discuss the best holiday that they could ever imagine—the place, the weather, what you would do, the hotel, travel, who goes with you and so on. Include your own idea of a dream holiday with them and why.

SAY The world is a wonderful place to live in but it can also be a difficult place at times—bad things can happen to people (relate to sin being a part of the world also). But heaven is a place that is so special that even the streets are made of gold! No one is sick there, or tired, no one grows old and we can get to enjoy God's company forever and ever. The best thing about following Jesus is that one day we will get to go to heaven—and God already has a room prepared there especially for us.

 "In my Father's house there are many dwelling-places." **John 14:2**

PRAY Lord God, you have prepared a place for us in heaven. Help us to live our lives every day knowing that we will be with you in heaven one day in the future. Amen.

MARK 16:15-16

PLAY! Place a glass of water in front of each person and discuss how many uses we have for water in the house (drinking, making dinner, cup of tea, hot water bottle, radiators, washing dishes and clothes, toilet, shower, watering plants and so on). What do you think would happen to all the plants (indoor and out) if there was no water? What would happen to animals and people? What would things look like if there were no water for washing?

SAY Water gives life. If we didn't drink water we would soon die. But water is also needed to make things clean again. Jesus taught us baptism as a symbol of a person deciding to follow him and asking for their sins to be forgiven. The water shows us that God has washed our sins away but it is also a symbol of the new life that we have when we become Christians. Some people get baptised as adults or young people but many do as babies, so their parents make the decision to follow Jesus on their behalf. Then, as they grow up, they can decide to follow Jesus for themselves.

 "Go into all the world and proclaim the good news to the whole creation." **Mark 16:15-16a**

PRAY Lord Jesus, baptism is about becoming part of your family. Thank you for our families— including our church family, because through baptism we are all joined together in you. Amen.

BIRTH

PSALM 139:13-16

 PLAY! Play a short baby animals quiz. What each of the following grows into and also how many babies each animal might usually have.

Puppy	Dog	6-10 puppies
Kitten	Cat	5-7 kittens
Chick	Hen	5-8 chicks
Calf	Cow	1 calf
Cub	Lion	2-4 cubs
Lamb	Sheep	1-3 lambs
Tadpole	Frog	1,000 eggs

SAY God is involved in making every baby animal but he takes great delight in making us. No matter what our size and shape, what colour we are, how we look, what we can and can't do—God made us. And from the moment a baby is born the Bible says that God knows every day that they will live and what they will do. So we are happy when a baby arrives, not just because they are such a gift but because God has great things planned for their lives.

 "In your book were written all the days that were formed for me, when none of them as yet existed." **Psalm 139:16b**

PRAY Thank you that you have known us from the very beginning, even before we were born. We pray that you will bless all babies, and help them to grow up knowing what great plans you have. Amen.

BIRTHDAYS

1 CORINTHIANS 1:4-5

PLAY! Do a review of the year. Get a photo of each person from around a year or so ago and ask what they think has changed. Do they look different? Have they learnt new things or had new experiences (holidays, new clubs/organisations, new things in school, changes in family, friends etc)?

 SAY Birthdays are a time to celebrate the wonderful gift of life that we have been given and a reminder that each child is a gift to their family not just on the day they were born but every day. This is one of the reasons why we give presents to someone on their birthday–to remind them that they are gift. A birthday is also a way to remember that another year in our life has passed and to thank God for it and also ask for his blessing for the year ahead..

"I give thanks to my God always for you because of the grace of God." **1 Corinthians 1:4a**

PRAY Thank you, God, for the lives you have given to us. When we celebrate our birthdays, help us to be really grateful for everything you have done for us and for everything you will do for us in the next year. Amen.

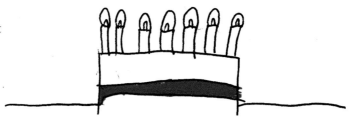

NEW YEAR AT SCHOOL / NEW SCHOOL

HOLIDAYS AND TRAVEL

PHILIPPIANS 4:12-13

PLAY! Hunt out a photo of you in a school uniform at a similar age to them. Encourage them to ask questions about what school was like for you such as the differences in how you learnt (no whiteboards!), the games you played at break, your favourite subjects and what you didn't like and were nervous about. Then ask them what some of their likes and dislikes about school are.

SAY Some children get very excited about a new term/teacher/school. Some children don't want to start back at all and would rather stay home! But school helps us to learn lots of important things and it can give us some good friends as well. So if you are a bit nervous of starting don't forget that you are not alone and that some other children are ready to be your friend, and that the teacher is there to help you. And if you are excited about starting then try and be a good friend to someone who isn't.

 "I can do all things through him who strengthens me." **Philippians 4:13**

PRAY Dear God, it can be really hard starting a new school or a new term. Give us strength to be brave and excited about the school year ahead, and to be there for other people who are nervous as well. Amen.

PSALM 139:7-10

PLAY! Get out a suitcase or travel bag and ask what some of the essential things that are needed for travel/holidays (clothing, snacks, money, tickets, map, medical, phone, sun cream, books, sunglasses etc). What have we forgotten? We haven't thought about packing any people! Why do we not need to pack any people? Do we need to pack God?

SAY It is really good to say thank-you to God for the opportunity to travel/go on holiday as we will see and experience new things and meet new people. It is also important to know that even though we can't pack God, as he will always be with us, we should still remember to pray to him, no matter where we are, and to ask for his protection for a safe journey.

 "If I settle at the farthest limits of the sea, even there your hand shall lead me, and your right hand shall hold me fast." **Psalm 139:9a-10**

PRAY Dear God, no matter where we go you are there. As we set out on a new journey, be with us as we travel, be with us when we get there and help us to enjoy our time together, knowing you are always with us. Amen.

VISITORS

ROMANS 12:9-13

 PLAY! In many parts of the world the arrival of a visitor is a big occasion. They may not have been seen for a while and might be hungry after a long journey so they are fed and looked after well. How might we treat visitors well (best food, drink, seats, best behaviour, comfort, sleeping arrangements etc)? How might a visitor feel if we didn't treat them well?

SAY How we welcome people is a very important part of being a Christian. God asks us to be very welcoming and friendly to people to show God's love and this is especially important if they come to our house. If we give them good food and the best seats and share things with them (such as toys) and are polite then this shows that God values them. This is why it is important to treat visitors well.

"Contribute to the needs of the saints; extend hospitality to strangers." **Romans 12:13**

 PRAY Dear Lord, thank you for these visitors to our home. Although sometimes this means things change for a short while, help us to be kind to our guests, just as we would like people to be kind to us. Amen.

SICKNESS

PSALM 147: 1-6

PLAY! If someone is sick in the house then make up a small basket or tray of things to help them and cheer them up. You could include a drink, book/comic, flowers, food, small present, picture, a small note or card and so on. Bring the items to them, and stay and pray with them. If someone else you know is sick then you could perhaps write a get-well card or note or even compose a text message to them.

SAY Sickness was not part of God's plan for creation and there is no sickness in heaven. We have sickness (along with other bad things) because it came to earth with the first sin of Adam and Eve. There will always be sickness in the world we live in and God sometimes will heal sickness–but even when he doesn't he will always be with us. It is important then to ask God to heal those that are sick and to comfort them. And for us to be happy–for when we get to heaven there will be no more sickness.

"He heals the broken-hearted, and binds up their wounds." **Psalm 147:3**

 **PRAY** Dear God, your Son Jesus healed so many people. He also knew what it was to feel pain and to suffer. We don't always know your plans for us, but we know you promise that one day we will be with you in heaven where there is no more sickness. Amen.

ANNIVERSARIES

MOTHERS/ FATHERS DAY

2 THESSALONIANS 2:15-17

PLAY! Play a cups game. Place three to four small cups, exactly the same, on the table and then place a small and soft item under one of them. Ask if it is easy to remember which cup hides the item. Then try and move the cups as quickly as possible to try and confuse them as to where it is hidden (you might have to try a few times if they are observant!). Ask why it was harder the second time round to remember where the item was.

SAY Even when something should be easy to remember, like an important event, it can be easy to forget because of other busy things that are happening. The reasons why we have anniversaries is to remember events in our lives. A birthday is a kind of an anniversary. What other anniversaries might there be (marriage, baptism, death, Easter, Christmas etc)? We use anniversaries to remember a date each year to remind us about something important and also to remember important things about God (e.g. Easter etc).

 "So then, brothers and sisters, stand firm and hold fast to the traditions that you were taught by us." **2 Thessalonians 2:15a**

 Lord Jesus, just as we celebrate important things in our lives, help us to celebrate other important things like Christmas and Easter, which remind us of the things you have done for us. Amen.

EPHESIANS 6:1-4

PLAY! Make up a 'how well do you know your mum/dad quiz'. Ask them various questions about mum/dad to see how they do. Their age, favourite food, TV show, hobbies, job, routine, middles name and so on. See how much they know. Then ask what they could do to give mum/dad a nice relaxing time for ten minutes (cup of tea, TV, feet up on sofa etc!) and see if they will do this at the end of the devotion!

SAY God gives children as gifts to mums and dads and mums and dads to children. It is important to remember that sometimes mums and dads can get very tired or fed up–and that it can be hard work to look after children. Mothers/ Fathers day is a special day to remind us how important they are. But should we only be nice to mum/dad one day per year? God wants children to help out and pray for their parents every day.

 "Children, obey your parents in the Lord, for this is right." **Eph 6:1**

 Dear Lord, thank you for the people who care for us, especially for our parents. Just as our parents want to do the best for us, help us to do the best we can as their children. Amen.

ADVENT

ISAIAH 7:14

PLAY! What sort of things do we think about coming up to Christmas (presents, decorations, holidays, parties etc)? Do we ever think about Christmas as a time for visitors? If I told you that someone very important like a Queen or President was coming to visit for a few days over Christmas what would you do (buy a present, tell people, get a room ready, tidy up and so on)? What would you do if Jesus was coming to stay?

SAY Advent is a time when we think about how Jesus came to be with us from heaven–as a little baby. Jesus was God coming to earth to be with us and if he was to come to our house as a person he would not be worried too much about us making the house ready–but getting our hearts ready. So advent is a time to think about Jesus coming into our lives and getting our hearts ready by saying sorry, praying and trying to be good

"Therefore the Lord himself will give you a sign. Look, the young woman is with child and shall bear a son, and shall name him Immanuel." **Isaiah 7:14**

PRAY Help us, O Lord, to prepare for Christmas by saying sorry for the bad things in our lives, so we can be even more ready for the wonderful gift of Christmas. Amen.

CHRISTMAS

LUKE 2:8-14

PLAY! 'Guess the decorations'. Take them to the Christmas tree and give them sixty seconds to look at everything on it and memorise what is there. Then turn them to face you (while you can still see the tree) and quiz them to see what they have remembered about the tree. Then they can all look at the tree again to see how they got on.

SAY Do you know why we decorate a Christmas tree? Not just to make the house look cheerful and as a place for presents but also to remind us of some of the important messages of Christmas.

The tree points towards God and its evergreen needles are a reminder of eternal life in heaven.
The lights symbolise Jesus as the light of the world.
The stars symbolize the star that the wise men followed to find Jesus.
The angels symbolize the angels that announced the birth of Jesus.
The colours red and green remind us of the blood of Jesus that would be spilt to save us and the everlasting life that would come from this.

"to you is born this day in the city of David a Saviour, who is the Messiah, the Lord." **Luke 2:11**

PRAY Lord God, when your Son came to be born in a stable, he became a human just like us, but without sin. Christmas means that you understand when we laugh, and when we cry. Help us to remember this and not be distracted by things like presents and sweets. Amen.

GOOD FRIDAY

LUKE 23:32-47

PLAY! Gather a candle and some matches and place them on the table. Then ask if they can think of any other names for Jesus (this will be hard). Explain that he was also called other names to describe what he was - such as the King of Kings, the Son of God and the Son of Man (as being both God and man) and Rabbi (teacher about God). He was also called two other names. Can you guess one if I do this (light the candle)?

SAY Jesus was also called the 'light of the world' (John 8:12) because he revealed to us what God was like and also the plan that he had to save us. He was also called our 'saviour'–because he came to save us from being dead forever. But on Good Friday he was arrested and then put to death on a cross. And as he was on the cross a darkness came over the whole land (blow out the candle). But did Jesus stay dead? We will find out on Sunday.

 "(Jesus) replied, 'Truly I tell you, today you will be with me in Paradise." **Luke 23:43**

PRAY Dear Lord, thank you that you went through so many bad things, even death, so that we can get to Heaven. Help us to remember all that you have done for us. In Jesus name, Amen.

EASTER

JOHN 3:16-17

PLAY! Play an Easter egg game. If you have some mini-eggs you could go on an egg hunt inside or outside the house. You could also get a chocolate egg (that is going to be eaten) and see how high you can drop it before it breaks (inside or outside the packaging).

SAY Easter Sunday is the most important day of the year for Christians. It is a celebration of the day that Jesus rose again from the dead, after being killed. Not just that he came alive again but that he had defeated the devil forever–so that we could have eternal life in heaven. An egg is a symbol of new life and we break eggs at Easter to remember that Jesus was once broken (on the cross) but that he came alive again to live for evermore.

 "For God so loved the world that he gave his only Son, so that everyone who believes in him may not perish but may have eternal life." **John 3:16**

PRAY Lord God, Easter is the most important day of the year. The first Easter was the most important day ever. Thank you for Jesus, who rose from the dead– for because of this we can look forward to heaven where we will be with you. Amen.

ALL SAINTS DAY / HALLOWEEN

EPHESIANS 5:8-10

 Make up a scary walk by placing a series of toys as 'monsters' around the floor and on tabletops with some 'treasure' beside them that they are guarding. Then blindfold one person and see if they think they can get the treasure without touching the monsters. Then pick someone else to be a 'saint' to guide them (by touch or by talking) to the treasure without touching the monsters. What was it like to have the saint with them?

 A saint is someone who faithfully follows Jesus and helps others to do so. It is not just a term for very important or famous Christians–all Christians are called saints. All Saints day is a day that remembers Christians everywhere but Halloween was thought superstitiously by some people to be the night before All Saints day as a time when all the bad things would come out - before they got banished on All Saints day. Today it is used by many people to dress up as scary things for fun.

 "For once you were darkness, but now in the Lord you are light. Live as children of light" **Ephesians 5:8**

 Lord God, it is so important for us to make sure that we have the right priorities in life. At Halloween, help us to remember that although dressing up can be fun, it is also a day that reminds us we are saints because of your light in our lives. Amen.

HARVEST

2 CORINTHIANS 9:10-11

 Get a variety of foodstuffs out from the cupboard, fridge etc and hide them under the table. Then reveal each, one at a time, and ask them to guess if they think each item is mostly from the ground (potatoes, carrots etc), trees (fruit, berries from bushes etc), animal (meat, cheese, milk etc) or sea (tins of tuna!). You can do this quickly for more fun if you like.

 Harvest is a special time when we thank God for providing for us and especially for the food we have to eat. God has given us food from the sea, animals, plants and trees and from the ground. Can you think of any other examples of food and where they are from? It is important that we are thankful and harvest is a good time to remind us to pray for farmers and fishermen who provide the food and for those people, all over the world, who struggle to get enough food to eat.

 "He who supplies seed to the sower and bread for food will… increase the harvest of your righteousness." **2 Corinthians 9:10**

 Dear Lord, thank you for farmers, fishermen and others who provide us with food to eat and enjoy. Thank you that every good thing comes first from you… help us to remember to say thank you every day for all the blessings you give us. Amen.

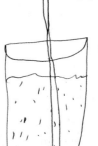

THE LORD'S PRAYER:

It is important to instill knowledge in children of The Lord's Prayer and the Ten Commandments. For if they know and remember these great foundations of teaching now then they will be able to relate to them throughout their life. So this section is for those who want to take their children a bit deeper in their understanding of faith. The Lord's Prayer is an important element of the Christian faith. A prayer that was given to us by Jesus as part of a great sermon he preached to his disciples from a mountainside and that is still taught today. It sums up how we should pray and relate to God every day. The Lord's Prayer can be found in Matthew 6.

THE LORD'S PRAYER

Our Father in heaven,
hallowed be your name,
your kingdom come,
your will be done,
on earth as in heaven.
Give us today our daily bread.
Forgive us our sins
as we forgive those who sin against us.
Lead us not into temptation
but deliver us from evil.
For the kingdom, the power,
and the glory are yours
now and for ever. Amen.

OUR FATHER IN HEAVEN, HALLOWED BE YOUR NAME

PLAY! 'Mirror faces'. Make a variety of different faces (such as cross, happy, surprised, disgusted, sad and so on) and see how quickly they can be mimicked by the children. Then get a small compact mirror and say (without revealing that it is a mirror) that there is a picture of one of God's children in it. Then show them their reflection.

SAY Did you know that God is also your Father because he created you? And each child is very special to him. God loves to see you, spend time with you and hear your prayers to him. In this prayer God is asking you to call him 'daddy' but also to remember that he is God, and is in heaven, so we should think of him as the most important thing there is.

 Each day of the devotions that focus on the Lord's Prayer, that should be the prayer you use with the children. It will help them to memorise the prayer (if they haven't already) but it will also make them familiar with it as they learn the meaning of its lines.

Our Father in heaven, hallowed be your name,

YOUR KINGDOM COME, YOUR WILL BE DONE, ON EARTH AS IT IS IN HEAVEN.

 Blindfold the children and then quickly set up a simple obstacle course across a few rooms by moving chairs, putting toys or cushions on the floor etc. Then ask each child to get from one part of the house to the other without standing on or hitting the obstacles. If they start to be hesitant about this then say that it is going to be OK because you are going to give them instructions and all they have to do is listen to them. Then complete the obstacle course.

SAY What did we have to do to be safe from the obstacles (obey the instructions)? This is the same with obeying God. In this prayer to God we are asking that his purpose be done in everything. That all good things that God makes happen in heaven will be done on earth—and that we might help to be part of it.

GIVE US THIS DAY OUR DAILY BREAD.

PLAY! Needs quiz. Do a quick quiz to see how many things that they can guess are essential for family life—perhaps offer a prize if they do well. A sample list could include; food, water, clothes, a house, heat, money, electricity, school, safety, sleep and so on.

SAY We need a lot more things than food don't we? This prayer is where we ask God for all our needs but not just for those that keep us fed, sheltered and safe. There are other needs that we should ask God to provide for us such as the need for friendship and the need for God to comfort us and to give us joy and laughter. What other things do you think we could ask God for?

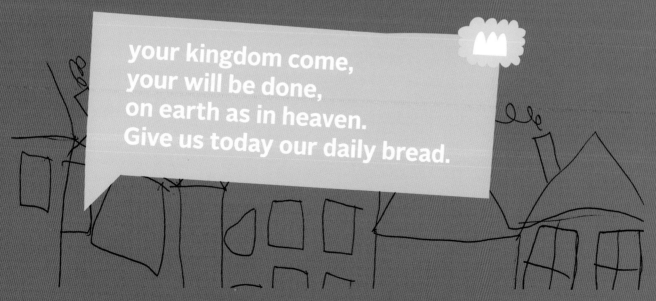

your kingdom come,
your will be done,
on earth as in heaven.
Give us today our daily bread.

FORGIVE US OUR SINS AS WE FORGIVE THOSE THAT SIN AGAINST US.

PLAY! Get a very small round stone or button (one for each child) and ask them how much they think it would hurt if it was dropped on their hand. Try this from varying heights (it should not hurt!). Then put the small stone in a shoe for each child and ask them to put the shoe on and go for a walk around the house. How does the stone feel now?

SAY This little stone doesn't seem like much but if you put it in a shoe then it becomes very uncomfortable. Whenever we do something wrong, even very small things, and don't say sorry then they become like that little stone and start to make our lives uncomfortable. This is why God asks us to come to him and say sorry–and he will forgive us (and take away the stone or sin). At the same time though he asks that we must also forgive those people who do wrong to us and then say sorry.

Forgive us our sins, as we forgive those who sin against us. Lead us not into temptation but deliver us from evil.

LEAD US NOT INTO TEMPTATION BUT DELIVER US FROM EVIL

PLAY! Set a really nice food treat in front of the children (perhaps some sweets on a plate) and tell them that they are not to touch it. Then make up an excuse to leave the room for a minute. Hopefully when you get back the treat will still be there but, if not, just include it as part of the talk!

SAY What are some of the naughty things that we do sometimes (disobeying parents, fighting, shouting, sulking, lying etc)? Do we want to be naughty or is it something that just happens often? The Bible says that there is someone called the devil, who doesn't like God, who tries to get us to do wrong things all the time and one of the ways that he does this is to tempt us. Is anyone here still thinking about the treat? What are you thinking? If you took it without permission would it be wrong? The devil tries to tempt us to do wrong things and so this prayer is to ask God to help protect us from temptation (you could finish by sharing the treat out!).

FOR THE KINGDOM, THE POWER AND THE GLORY ARE YOURS, NOW AND FOREVER. AMEN.

PLAY! Take everyone's pulses. To do this get everyone to place their middle two fingers on the inside of their wrist near the bone that leads to the thumb. Then get everyone to take each other's pulses. See who has the fastest and slowest pulse by counting the beats in 10 seconds and multiplying by six.

SAY God hears and knows every person's heartbeat. He also knows the number of hairs on our head. God knows everything, can do anything and be anywhere. This is why we say that this is his kingdom (he made it) and that he should be thanked for this forever. Even though there are bad things that happen in the world this is because people brought them here (relate to Adam and Eve) and God has decided that he would let us do what we want. But it is still God's world and heaven. Finally, we say 'Amen' at the end of a prayer as a way of saying to God 'So be it.'

For the kingdom, the power and the glory are yours, now and forever. Amen.

THE 10 COMMANDMENTS:

From the time that the very first sin separated mankind from God, He designed a plan to restore our relationship and fellowship with him. This plan was called a covenant and was to be shared with the whole world. The covenant meant that God's people would agree to obey a spoken and written set of obligations and responsibilities (laws) to demonstrate their devotion to God and separation from sin. At the very core of these laws were the 10 Commandments -a moral code given to Moses on two stone tablets on Mount Sinai after the people of Israel had been freed from Egypt.

The Commandments and other laws were designed to lead Israel to a life of practical holiness. In them, people could see the nature of God and his plan for how they should live. By Jesus' time however, many people looked at the laws the wrong way—they thought that to obey every law was to earn prosperity and protection from invasion or disaster. Law keeping became an end in itself and not the means to draw closer to God. Jesus pointed out that while the law was important in revealing who God is and how to follow him, it would ultimately be through Jesus that people would be restored to God. He had come to fulfill the Law and not abolish it. Therefore Christians regard both the Old and New Testament law highly.

1. You shall have no other gods before me

THE TEN COMMANDMENTS

1. You shall have no other gods before me
2. You shall not make for yourself an idol
3. You shall not misuse the name of the LORD your God
4. Remember the Sabbath by keeping it holy
5. Honour your father and mother
6. You shall not murder
7. You shall not commit adultery
8. You shall not steal
9. You shall not give false testimony
10. You shall not covet

1. YOU SHALL HAVE NO OTHER GODS BEFORE ME

PLAY! Discuss what it would be like to have another ten mums and dads. Would it be good or better? What things could they do? Could you get one to take you to school, one to make a nice lunch, one to help with homework, take you to the park, make dinner and so on? How would it make you feel? How do you think your mum and dad would feel about it?

SAY Your mum and dad love you so much that they would not want you to have another mum or dad that was more important than them. That's how God is too. He loves us so much that it hurts him if we decide to place anything else more important than him. That is why the first commandment says we should have no other gods.

PRAY *Great God, there is none like you. Be the most important thing in our lives. Amen.*

2. YOU SHALL NOT MAKE FOR YOURSELF AN IDOL

 Get them to list as many famous people that they can in sixty seconds (sports, talent shows, movies, magazines, TV and so on). Help suggest some of your own. Then discuss some of the examples and ask why they think they are famous (a talent or skill, someone that they are related/married to, money/business etc). If any of us were to be famous what do you think it would be for?

SAY Sometimes we get very excited about famous people and think that they are much better than everyone else because they are on TV. However, they are just like us and so it is important that we do not spend too much time thinking about them or their music or TV programmes. Just as God doesn't want us to have other gods he doesn't want us to have idols—which is thinking too much about other things or other people instead of God.

PRAY *Dear God you are everything we need. Don't let us be distracted by other things. Amen.*

3. YOU SHALL NOT MISUSE THE NAME OF THE LORD YOUR GOD

PLAY! Ask if they have ever heard anyone say a bad word (but not to repeat it!). Does their teacher ever tell anyone off for saying bad words? When might someone use a bad word (when annoyed, angry, hurt, surprised, trying to be rude etc)? We are going to pretend now that your name is a bad word. (Then pretend that you have hurt yourself and say, in a cross voice, 'their name' as a bad word. Do this for everyone). How does it feel to have your name used this way? Would you like everyone to use your name as a bad word?

SAY Often people say 'God' or 'Jesus' as bad words. This is usually because they have learnt it from others as they have grown up and don't realise what they are doing. However, it is still a wrong thing to do as it hurts God. You see God is so important that his names are very important too (just like how our names are important) and this is why we should not misuse them.

PRAY *Dear Jesus, your name is more precious than gold. May we never use it the wrong way. Amen.*

2. You shall not make for yourself an idol

3. You shall not misuse the name of the LORD your God

4. REMEMBER THE SABBATH BY KEEPING IT HOLY

PLAY! Do some running on the spot as fast as you can and see if you can count to twenty (Or sooner if they tire). Once everyone is tired then sit down and ask why we couldn't keep going. Rest for a bit longer and then start again but this time count to six and then stop for two to three deep breaths and then start again and count to seven. Then start again and see if you can repeat this two to three times. Ask at the end what is easiest, running without stops or running with rests? Why?

SAY God made everything in creation in six days but on the seventh day (called Sunday) he rested. He gave us Sunday (the Sabbath) so we could rest too and not get tired out. But he also gave us the Sabbath to help us remember him and that is why we should treat it as a holy or special day dedicated to God. What might we do on a Sunday to keep it holy (go to church, pray together, rest, have fun, not work)?

PRAY *God above, you gave us enough time to spend lots of it with you. Help us to use it well. Amen.*

5. HONOUR YOUR FATHER AND MOTHER

PLAY! Imagine you are mum or dad. What are the most important jobs that you will have to do (feed, tidy-up, work, take care of children, homework help, school stuff, teaching things and so on and so on!)? What do you think are the hardest of these jobs?

SAY God gave children their parents so that they would be looked after and taught lots of things—especially about God. But God knows that it is hard to be a parent sometimes and that is why he commands us to honour and obey our mum and dad—to help them. Now sometimes it is hard to do the things that parents ask and sometimes they ask things that don't seem fair but God says it is important though and that he will bless us if we do this.

PRAY *Dear God, our parents are very special and important. Help us to love them and show them how we love them. Amen.*

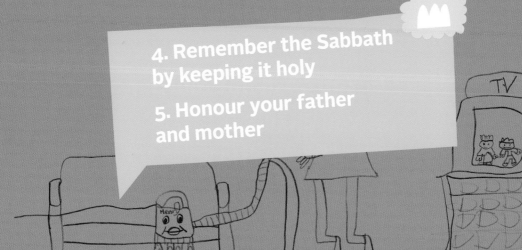

4. Remember the Sabbath by keeping it holy

5. Honour your father and mother

6. YOU SHALL NOT MURDER

 If there are three or more of you then play 'murder wink'. Place each person at different corners of the room/table so that each person can see the faces of the others. Then tell them that when they are winked at (by you) they have to die as theatrically as possible. Try it a few times and then play it with everyone's eyes closed at the start while you touch someone to be the 'killer'. Then, when they open their eyes they will not know who is the person that will wink to 'murder' them.

SAY God gave us life and made all of our lives very precious. So he commands us not to kill or harm each other. He also wants us to think about how we can try and protect other people from harm and from hurt and to help those, like the police, who are here to protect us.

PRAY *Dear God, you give us lives that are special. Help us see how special others are and be kind to them. Amen.*

7. YOU SHALL NOT COMMIT ADULTERY

PLAY! Place on the table as many of the following items as possible: A ring, banknote, Bible and something with lots of colours (preferable rainbow coloured). Ask what they are and what they all have in common? They can all be used as symbols of a promise. The ring as part of marriage, the banknote to pay money (it may say 'promise to pay the bearer...'), the Bible can be used to swear a promise and the rainbow is a reminder of God's promise not to flood the earth again. What else might we do to show a promise?

 Promises are very important to God and we shouldn't make any unless we intend to keep them. God says that getting married to someone is one of the most important promises we make and when someone commits adultery they break that promise and sometimes the marriage is finished. This commandment from God is also a reminder of the importance of commitment–not just in marriages but to family and friends too.

PRAY *God of love, you call us to care for others. Help us to be committed to this with our family and friends. Amen.*

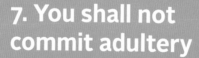

6. You shall not murder

7. You shall not commit adultery

8. YOU SHALL NOT STEAL

 Get everyone to go and get their favourite toy/possession and set it on the table. Then ask them to go and get a favourite book/other possession. When they are away hide all their favourite things on the table and when they come back say that you think they might have been stolen. Make sure they understand that you are joking. Ask how they would feel if someone actually did come into the house and steal these things and other items. Return them at the end of the talk.

SAY Most people get things because they have worked to get them or have been given them. But some people steal things and this is a bad thing to do. What do you think often gets stolen (money, possessions, cars, jewellery, clothes etc)? Did you know that stealing can also be taking small things off people like toys, pencils, sharpeners and so on without asking? God says that we should not steal anything–no matter how small.

PRAY *Dear God, you have given us many good things. Help us not to take things that aren't ours. Amen.*

9. YOU SHALL NOT GIVE FALSE TESTIMONY

PLAY! Make up a story about the day so far (or about your plans for tomorrow). Keep the story mostly truthful but change some key facts to see if they can be spotted. For instance change the times, locations, deeds, food eaten, names and so on. Ask if they can identify the lies in the story.

SAY False testimony is when we don't tell the truth about ourselves or other people (like the story) or when we tell a lie about something to try and not get into trouble. Can you think of any examples when you lied because you thought you might get into trouble (share examples from your own life)? God says that we should tell the truth because it will be better for us.

 Heavenly Father, you are a God of truth. Help us be truthful in our lives. Amen.

10. YOU SHALL NOT COVET

PLAY! Explain that, because they have reached the end of the Ten Commandments, that they are going to get a sweet. Then make a show of giving each child one sweet and keep the rest in a pile for yourself. While your pile of sweets is sitting in front of you ask them if they know of anyone they know that has a toy or game that they would like. What is it and why would they like it? Is there anything on the table that they would like (sweets)? Make the point though that they are yours but then share some more anyway before putting away.

SAY To covet is to keep thinking about other people's possessions and to want them for ourselves. Do you think it would be a good idea to always want something that we don't have? Would it say that we are happy with what we already own or that we wanted more? God has blessed us with many things and he wants us to be thankful and happy (but this isn't possible when we are ungrateful) so he commands us to try and not covet other people's things.

 Dear God, you meet all our needs. Help us not to be jealous of others. Amen.

 10. You shall not covet

Acknowledgements:

So many people have played a part in the formation of this book that it would not be possible to name them all. Those that can be named are:

Andi McCarroll, **Adrian Dorrian and The Down and Dromore people**

Youth and Children's Groups: Martin, Craig, Peter, Rachel, Natalie, Simon, Bryan, Dave, Lynne, Angela, Stephen and Matt.

Children's Officer: Julie Currie

Office: Mary, Margaret, Philip and Annette

Website Designer: Martin Montgomery

Bishop Harold Miller, Stephen Doherty, Peter Hilton, Simon Henry, Judith Cairns, Sharon Hamill and Helen Warnock

Church of Ireland Literature Committee

My Wife and family

Our Lord and Saviour Jesus Christ.

Christian Focus Publications

Christian Focus Publications publishes books for adults and children under its four main imprints: Christian Focus, CF4K, Mentor and Christian Heritage.

Our books reflect our conviction that God's Word is reliable and Jesus is the way to know him, and live for ever with him.

Our children's publication list includes a Sunday School curriculum that covers pre-school to early teens, and puzzle and activity books. We also publish personal and family devotional titles, biographies and inspirational stories that children will love.

If you are looking for quality Bible teaching for children then we have an excellent range of Bible stories and age-specific theological books.

From pre-school board books to teenage apologetics, we have it covered!
Find us at:
www.christianfocus.com

CF4∙K
Because you're never
too young to know Jesus

10 9 8 7 6 5 4 3 2 1
Copyright © 2015 Andrew Brannigan
ISBN: 978-1-78191-589-9
Published in 2015 by Christian Focus Publications Ltd.
Geanies House, Fearn, Tain, Ross-shire, IV20 1TW, Great Britain
Cover design by Daniel Van Straaten.

For Mum and Dad ..who did a good job and for Emily, Elizabeth, Grace and Lily ... who some day will